W9-BAP-106

Baby Animals

Marfé Ferguson Delano

NATIONAL
GEOGRAPHIC
KiDS

WASHINGTON, D.C.

Look, a baby!

Some babies snuggle on snowy sheets of ice.

Some babies cuddle
in warm, cozy dens.

Others live in nests high in trees.

Some babies toddle and trot on grassy hills and plains.

Splash!

And some swim and
leap through wavy seas.

Mmm! A moth makes a fine meal for a baby bird.

Which would you rather eat: fish, worms, or bugs?

Feed me!

All baby animals have to eat to grow, just like you. Baby birds gobble up food their parents bring to them, such as tasty bugs or fish.

How wide can you open your mouth?

This bird is bringing its chicks a yummy frog dinner!

Open wide for a delicious bug!

Some baby animals are called mammals. They drink milk from their mother. Bears, cheetahs, and whales are mammals. So are humans.

Let's rub noses! Orca babies stay close to their moms.

How many cheetah cubs do you see in this picture?

This mama bear has three cubs to feed. How many children are in your family?

Some baby animals can walk soon after they're born.

Some need a lift
from mom or dad.

Boing! Boing! Boing! Can you jump like a wallaby?

Hang on!

Some babies bounce along, snug in mother's pouch.

Other babies have to hang on tight!

Bath time!

Mother elephants give their babies dust baths! The dirt helps protect their skin.

How do you keep your skin and hair clean?

When you were a baby, your parents kept you neat and clean. They bathed you and washed your hair. Some animal parents keep their babies tidy, too. But you might be surprised by how they do it!

To keep her baby clean, a monkey mom picks dirt and insects off its skin and fur.

How do you think it would feel to be licked by a mountain lion?

A mountain lion mother uses her tongue instead of a washcloth to clean her cub.

Baby animals have a lot to learn, from jumping to climbing ...

Baby bears
have sharp claws
that help them grip
tree trunks. Have
you ever climbed
a tree?

How high can
you climb?
As high as these
baby bears?

... from swimming to flying!

What do you think this water feels like? Would you like to swim in it?

Ready, set, flap! This eagle chick is testing its wings, practicing for the day it will fly out of the nest.

It's playtime! Some babies swing and scamper through trees.

Growl!

Some baby animals pretend to fight. They tumble and tussle and wrestle and bite. Pretend fighting helps baby animals learn to hunt!

My turn!

How do you think this baby elephant brings grass to its mouth?

As they grow older, baby animals learn to find food for themselves. Some babies watch and copy their mother as she eats grass, leaves, or fruit.

How high can you stretch your neck? High enough to reach juicy leaves?

Others learn to dig for worms or bugs. Some mother animals teach their babies how to catch fish or hunt.

This young fox caught a mouse dinner all by itself!

Meerkat parents teach their babies how to scratch in the dirt to find insects to eat.

"Hey, Mom, what are we hunting for? Seals again?"

The world is full of
things for babies
to explore—to sniff
and touch and taste!

Ah, there's nothing like a sweet-smelling flower! Do you like to smell flowers?

Shhh!

All that learning and playing and exploring can make a baby tired. Baby animals need their sleep—just like you.

The Name Game!

Some baby animals are called by special names. For example, a baby penguin is called a chick. Baby goats are called kids. Here are some more baby animals, with their special names. Can you say what the grown-up animals are called?

a. Calf

b. Foal

c. Joey

d. Fawn

e. Cub

f. Owlet

Answer key: a. Elephant;
b. Zebra; c. Kangaroo;
d. Deer; e. Lion; f. Owl

31

For my wise and beautiful mother, Marie Ferguson —MFD

Copyright © 2015 National Geographic Society
Published by the National Geographic Society
Washington, D.C. 20036

All rights reserved. Reproduction of the whole or any part of the contents without written permission from the publisher is prohibited.

Editor: Ariane Szu-Tu
Art Director: Amanda Larsen
Designer: Callie Broaddus
Photography Editor: Lori Epstein

National Geographic supports K–12 educators with ELA Common Core Resources. Visit www.natgeoed.org/commoncore for more information.

Trade paperback ISBN: 978-1-4263-2046-0
Reinforced library binding ISBN: 978-1-4263-2047-7

The publisher gratefully acknowledges zoologist Lucy Spelman, D.V.M., and National Geographic's early childhood development specialist Catherine D. Hughes for their expert review of the book.

ILLUSTRATIONS CREDITS

Cover, Ferrero-Labat/ARDEA; back cover, Eric Isselee/Shutterstock; 1, David Rasmus/Shutterstock; 2-3, Daniel J. Cox/NaturalExposures.com; 4-5, Norbert Rosing/National Geographic Creative; 6 (both), Suzi Eszterhas/Minden Pictures; 7, wizdata/Shutterstock; 8, ZSSD/Minden Pictures; 9 (UP), Wild Horizons/UIG/Getty Images; 9 (LO), Hans Leijnse/Minden Pictures; 10 (UP), stockoftor2321/iStockphoto; 10 (CTR), Ozerov Alexander/Shutterstock; 10 (LO), Porojnicu Stelian/Shutterstock; 11 (UP), Hiroya Minakuchi/Minden Pictures; 11 (CTR), Suzi Eszterhas/Minden Pictures; 11 (LO), Photodisc/Getty Images; 12 (LE), Janugio/iStockphoto; 12 (RT), pjmalsbury/iStockphoto; 13, Denis-Huot/Nature Picture Library; 14, Dave Watts/Minden Pictures; 15 (UP), Christian Ziegler/Minden Pictures; 15 (LO), Mark Higgins/iStockphoto; 16 (UP), imageBROKER/Alamy; 16 (LO), tratong/Shutterstock; 17, Panoramic Images/Getty Images; 18, Charlie Summers/Nature Picture Library; 19, Erik Mandre/Shutterstock; 20 (UP), Flip Nicklin/National Geographic Creative; 20 (LO), Michio Hoshino/Minden Pictures; 21, Roland Seitre/Nature Picture Library; 22, salajean/Shutterstock; 23 (UP), tiger cubs playing/Shutterstock; 23 (LO), Sergey Gorshkov/Minden Pictures; 24 (UP), Maggy Meyer/Shutterstock; 24 (LORT), Mitsuaki Iwago/Minden Pictures; 24 (LOLE), Madlen/Shutterstock; 25 (UP), Bildagentur Zoonar GmbH/Shutterstock; 25 (CTR), Scott Boulton/Alamy; 25 (LO), Jan Vermeer/Minden Pictures; 26 (UP), Julie Lubick/Shutterstock; 26 (LE), Chris Johns/National Geographic Creative; 26 (RT), Tim Fitzharris/Minden Pictures; 27, Gary Vestal/Photographer's Choice/Getty Images; 28-29, Terry Wilson/E+/Getty Images; 30 (UP), Richard Du Toit/Minden Pictures; 30 (LO), Kjuuurs/Shutterstock; 30 (RT), Francois van Heerden/iStockphoto; 31 (UPLE), Tammy Wolfe/iStockphoto; 31 (UPRT), Dave Pusey/Shutterstock; 31 (LO), MarkBridger/Flickr Open/Getty Images; 32, Jjustas/Shutterstock

ANIMAL NAMES BY PAGE NUMBER

Front cover: African elephants
Back cover: koalas
Page 1: brown bears
Page 2: gray wolf
Pages 4-5: polar bears
Page 6 (top): coyotes
Page 6 (bottom): spotted hyenas
Page 8: white rhinoceros
Page 9 (top): bottlenose dolphins
Page 9 (bottom): manatees
Page 10 (top): moth
Page 10 (middle): starlings
Page 10 (bottom): terns
Page 11 (bottom): brown bears
Page 12 (left): giraffes
Page 12 (right): zebra
Page 13: African lions
Page 15 (top): three-toed sloths
Page 15 (bottom): chimpanzees
Page 19: brown bears
Page 20 (top): humpback whales
Page 20 (bottom): harp seals
Page 21: Spanish imperial eagle
Page 22: macaque
Page 23 (top): tigers
Page 23 (bottom): Arctic foxes
Page 24 (bottom): giraffes
Page 25 (top): Cape fox
Page 25 (bottom): polar bears
Page 26 (top): moose
Page 26 (bottom left): alligators
Page 26 (bottom right): red fox
Page 27: giant panda
Pages 28-29: deer
Page 32: snails

Printed in Hong Kong
15/THK/1